FOOD *for* BRACES

Recipes and Food Ideas
What to Eat in the First Week
Lunch Box Solutions
What Foods to Avoid
Tips for Eating Out
Sample Meal Plans

By Suzanne Burke

Originally published through IngramSpark 2022.

Paperback ISBN 978-0-6483205-1-7
E-book ISBN 978-0-6483205-2-4

Website: www.foodforbraces.com
Email: info@foodforbraces.com

Join the Facebook Community Group where we share food ideas and stories about eating with braces:
https://www.facebook.com/groups/foodforbracescommunity

© 2022 Copyright Suzanne Burke. All rights reserved.
No part of this publication may be, stored in a retrieval system or transmitted in any form by any means, electronic or mechanical, recording, scanning or otherwise without the prior written permission of the author

Disclaimer – Important PLEASE READ

The information presented within this book is the author's opinion and does not constitute any health or medical advice. The content of this book is for informational purposes only.

Please seek advice from your healthcare provider for your personal health concerns prior to acting on any of the information in this book.
This book is not a replacement for advice from your orthodontist, dentist, dietician or any other health professional. All recipes and food recommendations have been made with the purpose of providing you with fun and interesting food ideas and for general information purposes only.

Dietary recommendations are healthy for the majority of people but potentially dangerous for others. You are responsible for your own health and safety at all times. By continuing to read this book beyond this page you acknowledge and agree to the above and the following:

- You have been assessed and are under the care of a qualified professional for your braces and dental health management.
- You are responsible for your own diet choices. In particular, if you have any special dietary needs or medical conditions that require a special diet, that you have consulted a health professional.
- This book does not provide medical advice. Where there is a conflict between the information in this book and the advice provided by your health care provider(s), then the advice of the health care provider should be followed.
- All material provided in this book and associated website, including text, images, graphics, photos and anything else, are all provides for informational purposes only are not a substitute for medical advice or treatment.
- You acknowledge and understand that sugar can be harmful to your teeth and consuming too much sugar can lead to build of plaque on your teeth & lead to teeth decay. You are responsible for ensuring that you consume sugar in moderation. If in doubt as to what is an acceptable level of sugar in your diet, consult a health professional to seek advice.
- The author and or publishers are not responsible for any recipes that you cook that fail! While every effort has gone into providing high quality content, even the simplest of recipes can fail!

TABLE OF CONTENTS

Why was this book written?... 1
    Who is this book for? 2
    What will you get out of this book? 3
    So, you have braces. Now what? 4

Your First Week wearing Braces 6
    What to Eat in the First Week 7
    Food Ideas for the First Week of Wearing Braces 9
    Breakfast Ideas for the First Week 10
    Lunch and Dinner Ideas for the First Week 11
    Dessert Ideas for the First Week 12
    What to Eat AFTER the First Week 13

Types of Foods to Avoid.. 19
    Avoiding Hard or Crunchy Foods 20
    Avoiding Sticky or Chewy Foods 21
    What is Teeny Weeny Food 22
    Spicy Food and why you need to be careful 23
    'Big Bite' Food! Avoid braces busters! 24
    Food that Stains that you need to avoid 25
    List of foods that stain braces 27

Your Handy Checklist of FOODS to Avoid while wearing Braces.............................. 28
Non-Food Things to avoid chewing on... 29
Foods that are your Friend... 30
    Meat and Protein 30
    Vegetables.. 31
    Fruit 32
    Carbohydrates 33

Breakfast Ideas and Recipes.. 34
    Apple Puree – perfect soft food 34
    Banana and Cinnamon mash – fast and easy.. 35
    Breakfast Smoothies!!! 36
    Breakfast Smoothies!!! All the Colours of the RAINBOW! 37
    Scrambled Eggs – a great protein source 38
    Tofu Scramble – great for vegetarians/vegans 39
    Pancakes – a family favourite 40

TABLE OF CONTENTS

Pikelets - brilliant snacks and lunch box fillers 41
Creamy Mushroom Open Sandwich - Yum! 42
Muffins – the perfect brunch or lunchbox food 43
Pear and Dark Chocolate Muffins - crowd-pleaser! 44

Lunch and Dinner Recipes 46

Mashed potatoes - your secret weapon 46
Cauliflower Cheese - a family favourite 48
Guacamole – Good Old Smashed Avo! 50
Potato Salad – brilliant side dish or lunch box filler 51
Lettuce and Blue Cheese salad - tasty lunch or side dish 52
Fish Patties - simply delicious 53
Potato and Leek Soup - smooth and satisfying 55
Fish Chowder - so tasty! 57
Corn Chowder - great comfort food 59
Chicken Noodle Soup - Soul food! 61
Baked Salmon with steamed vegies 63
Creamy Salmon and Pea Pasta - a taste sensation! 64
Chicken and Noodle Stir-fry 66
Meatloaf - great as tasty leftovers in lunchboxes! 68
Savoury Mince - a hearty winter warmer 70
Cottage Pie – classic comfort food 72
Pulled Pork – a Slow Cooker Favourite 73
Roasted Sweet Potato, Feta and Basil Pasta Salad 75
Bocconcini and fresh tomato pasta salad 77

DESSERT Recipes 79

Cottage cheese and chopped fruit – fast and easy 79
Stewed Fruit – great for dessert or breakfast 80
Smooth Banana Dessert Bowl - a sweet delight 81
Soft Cookies – cookie treats that won't break braces! 82
Apple Crumble - great for all the family to enjoy 84
Self-Saucing Chocolate Pudding – chocolate heaven 86
Apple Pudding - You will be going back for seconds! 88
Pear Clafoutis - sophisticated and delicious 90

TABLE OF CONTENTS

EASY Lunchbox Solutions 92
    Sandwiches 93
    Use your dinner leftovers 94

Tips for Eating Out AND Ordering Take-away 95
    Going out for Breakfast or Brunch 95
    Breakfast and Brunch are full of great options. 95
    Japanese Food – tasty but can be sticky 96
    Burger Joints – avoid braces busters! 97
    Pizza – Eating out and Take-away 98
    Italian Food – creamy pastas are perfect 99
    Chinese Food – lots of great options 100
    Indian Food can be tricky 101
    Thai Food – some great tasty options 102
    American Food – avoid big bites! 103
    Fast Food – What to Eat and What to Avoid 104
    Eating Out and Choosing Desserts 105

Can I Eat that? Your Frequently Asked Questions 106
    Can you eat popcorn with braces? 107
    Can you eat chips with braces? 108
    Can you eat chocolate with braces? 109
    Can you eat ice cream with braces? 110
    What candy / lollies can you eat with braces? 111
    Can you eat cereal with braces? 112
    Can you drink coffee with braces? 113
    Can you eat marshmallows with braces? 114
    Can you eat peanut butter and/or jam/jelly with braces? 115
    Can you eat rice with braces? 116
    Can you eat bread with braces? 117
    Can you eat goldfish with braces? 118

Tempting Fussy Eaters 119
    9 Winning Ideas for tempting fussy eaters 120
    My Philosophy on keeping family harmony at mealtimes 123

Sample Meal Plan – First Week Of Braces 124
Sample Meal Plan – After First Week Of Braces 125

FOOD *for* BRACES

Why was this book written?

As an avid foodie, I found that when the time came for my children to wear braces, there was truly little information about how to make fun, interesting and yummy food. Most of the available information came in the form of orthodontic brochures or sensible health-related websites. While these serve an important purpose, they were lacking in practical information for fun meals and family meals.

In particular, I wanted to know how to help my kids survive the first week of braces and how to pack a yummy lunch box that wouldn't be a braces buster! My kids are both done and dusted with braces now (and yes it was worth it!), so I decided to put pen to paper and share what I learnt along the way.

Who is this book for?

This book is suitable for anyone with dental braces, on a soft food diet, after having wisdom teeth removed and after any major dental work such as tooth extractions. This includes:

- √ Anyone who has or is getting braces
- √ Parents of children with braces
- √ Anyone with soft-food requirements e.g. people with sensitive teeth or problems chewing
- √ Anyone that has had or is planning major dental work e.g. wisdom teeth removal, root canals

FOOD *for* BRACES

What will you get out of this book?

This book is full of great ideas and recipes for cooking 'braces-friendly' food. That is, food that won't break your braces (which means an unscheduled trip to your Orthodontist), food that won't stain your braces, food that is easy to prepare, easy to eat and best of all, food that is yummy!

So, you have braces. Now what?

When your teeth and gums are feeling sensitive, you will need some food options that are easy to eat. This book provides options for a range of soft food options. Some will not require any chewing at all such as soups and smoothies and these are perfect for when you are feeling the most sensitive. There is also a wide range of options and ideas for when your teeth have settled, but you still require relatively soft food to prevent braces breakage.

FOOD FOR SENSITIVE GUMS

Nearly all the food in this book is non-spicy and non-acidic. This means that sore gums and ulcers in your mouth will not sting or feel uncomfortable when eating.

NON-STAINING FOOD

Braces (particularly ceramic) and the teeth underneath can stain easily with certain types of food. I have included many recommendations for food to avoid and better still, lots of options for food that won't cause staining issues.

GETTING FOOD STUCK

You will need to avoid food that will get stuck in your braces as this may lead to tooth decay and other problems. This book includes lots of tips for the typed of food to avoid that will get stuck such as small seeds and gummy lollies.

This book is here to help you

Ultimately, the purpose of this book is to help you find some favourite foods that will become your 'go-to' food to enjoy while you are on your braces journey. Remember, getting braces is only for a brief period in your life and at the end of the process you will have beautifully aligned teeth and a beautiful smile to be proud of.

This book will help you enjoy your braces journey with some wonderful food. I hope you enjoy the book!

FOOD for BRACES

Your First Week wearing BRACES

In the first week after getting your braces and immediately after each adjustment, you will need to eat FIRST WEEK food. These are foods that you can eat with minimal or no chewing.

Great examples of FIRST WEEK food for braces include simple stuff like yoghurt, soups, smoothies, ice-cream, custard, etc...

FOOD *for* BRACES

What to Eat in the First Week

The first week of braces will take a bit of adjustment for most people. There will be some discomfort as you adjust to the feeling of the hardware in your mouth. There will be soreness as the teeth are starting to be gently maneuvered towards their new position.

In the first few days or even for the entire first week you may want to avoid chewing at all. To start with, you will need to consider options such as pureed food which can just be spooned in with no chewing required. While initially that thought can sounds disgusting it does not have to be disgusting at all. You can drink some delicious smoothies, have some nutritious and filling soups and much more.

FOOD *for* BRACES

As each day goes by you can introduce soft foods with a bit more substance and slowly introduce more solid foods that only require a small amount of chewing. Before too long you will be effectively eating normally again.

However, going back to normal eating will require some adjustments. There will now be a list of foods that are off limits so that you can avoid breaking your braces. Remember this is only while you are wearing braces and that is not forever. Most people wear braces for 12 to 18 months, so whatever you have go without, just remember it is only for a short time! You can do this!

Focus on what you CAN eat instead of what you are missing out on. There are a lot of delicious foods available for you to eat. Get creative in the kitchen and put your own twist on some of the ideas I have listed for you here!

Food Ideas for the First Week of Wearing Braces

Store Bought Stuff - Easy Options for the First Week
- Ice-cream
- Chocolate Mouse
- Crème Caramel
- Jelly
- Custard
- Pre-made soups (smooth only or puree yourself)

Breakfast Ideas for the First Week

- Soft, stewed or mashed fruit e.g. apples, bananas
- Smoothies – strawberry, blueberry, vanilla, mango, banana
- Scrambled eggs
- Yoghurt
- Porridge
- Softened cereal

FOOD *for* BRACES

Lunch and Dinner Ideas for the First Week

- Soup – potato, vegetable, pumpkin Homemade Chicken Noodle Soup
- Fish Chowder
- Mashed potatoes with gravy and mushrooms
- Fish patties
- Salmon and Pea pasta
- Roasted Vegies (soft only, not fibrous)
- Mild Mexican beans
- Chicken and Corn Chowder
- Meatloaf
- Pulled pork
- Baked salmon or poached fish
- Steamed or boiled vegetables (add butter, salt and pepper to taste

Dessert Ideas for the First Week

- Ice creams (no nuts)
- Jelly
- Custard
- Chocolate Mousse
- Pannacotta

What to Eat AFTER the First Week

Here are some ideas for soft and easy to eat food that you should be able to eat without any problem while you are wearing braces. Many of these food ideas are in the recipe section too.

Breakfast food ideas for after the first week
- Pancakes
- French Toast
- Toast without crust with mushrooms and sour cream
- Mashed Avo on soft Bread such as brioche
- Muffins
- Waffles

Lunch Ideas for after the first week

- Soft bread sandwiches without crusts. Sandwich filling ideas:
    - o Chopped boiled egg
    - o Thinly sliced ham and tomato
    - o Hummus
- Potato salad
- Macaroni cheese

Dinner Ideas for after the first week

- Best protein sources – your softest options are lentils, beans, tofu, fish, chicken, slow- cooked meat
- Pasta bake
- Shepherd's Pie / Cottage Pie
- Chicken Pie
- Pan-fried salmon and sweet potato mash
- Filled pasta such as Ravioli and Tortellini with a creamy sauce
- Soft Noodles e.g. egg noodles, udon, rice noodles
- Soft nachos – use cut up pita bread instead of corn chips
- Slow cooked meat – lamb shanks, pulled pork
- Risotto

Salad and Vegetables for eating after the first week

- Shredded lettuce
- Guacamole
- Boiled and steamed vegetables – soft only
- Mashed potatoes
- Potato salad
- Pasta salad
- Cauliflower cheese

Food for BRACES

Dessert ideas for eating after the first week

- Apple Crumble
- Custard and strawberries
- Jelly, custard, chocolate mousse layer sundae!
- Trifle in a cup or sponge cake with custard
- Chocolate cake
- Chocolate Pudding
- Chocolate mousse

FOOD for BRACES

Snacks for eating on the run or Quick Bites

- Muffins – pear and dark chocolate
- Soft fruit – kiwi, banana, rockmelon, seedless grapes
- Chocolate Pudding
- Cake and cupcakes and muffins
- Carrot and apple cake (no nuts)
- Ice-cream
- Soft cookies
- Hash Browns
- Apple sauce
- Bananas

FOOD *for* BRACES

Types of Foods to Avoid

Some foods can break the braces brackets and others can stick so badly to the braces that they can be a cleaning nightmare. Other food such as small seeds can get so embedded that it may be near on impossible to remove the seeds. Other foods can stain your teeth. If you have ceramic braces, these can also get stained.

You will need to avoid food that will:
- Break your braces
- Get stuck in your braces
- Hurt inflamed gums or irritate ulcers
- Stain your teeth and/or stain ceramic braces

Food that are bad for your braces fall into these main categories:
- × Hard or Crunchy
- × Sticky or Chewy
- × Teeny Weeny Food Spicy
- × Big bite food
- × Food that Stains

Chilli can sting sensitive gums

Suzanne Burke | www.foodforbraces.com

Avoiding Hard or Crunchy Foods

Hard or crunchy foods to avoid include corn chips (bye bye nachos for a while), nuts or anything nutty such as granola, popcorn and raw vegetables such as carrots.

FOOD *for* BRACES

Avoiding Sticky or Chewy Foods

Sticky food such as lollies/candy will get stuck in your braces and cause a terrible mess. Some lollies will feel like glue on your braces, some will cause breakage and some will be seemingly impossible to pick out and clean afterwards. They are best avoided.

Typical examples of sticky food to avoid includes chewing gum, fantails, minties and toffees and any other sticky lollies.

No Chewing Gum!

What is Teeny Weeny Food

Tiny little things can cause the most problems sometimes. The food that I put in the teeny-weeny category are small seeds and grains such as poppy seeds, sesame seeds and grains such as quinoa. These can get caught underneath your braces and be ever so difficult to pick out. They are best avoided.

Avoid Seeds

Food for Braces

Spicy Food and why you need to be careful

Avoid spicy food if you have inflamed gums as these may cause discomfort. Spicy foods include curries, anything containing chilli and anything acidic such as salad dressing containing lemon juice.

Yellow curries can cause staining

'Big Bite' Food! Avoid braces busters!

Food such as hamburgers that you sink your teeth into with a 'big bite' are off the menu, well sort of! You can still eat this type of food, but you will need to be careful. It is recommended that you cut 'big food' it into small pieces first.

Essentially, any food that requires you to take a big bite using your front teeth, is likely to damage the braces on the front teeth. Typical food that falls into this category are apples, hamburgers, hotdogs, corn on the cob, ribs, chicken drumsticks.

Instead, cut big-bite food into smaller pieces so your teeth do not need to do all the hard work. With apples you can cut them into slices. With a burger or other food that requires a lot of big bites, you need to use a knife and fork to chop it into smaller pieces. If you don't want to do this, then you might need to go without a hamburger for a while!

Avoid Corn on the cob. Biting into it will break your braces.

Food *for* BRACES

Food that Stains that you need to avoid

Certain foods that are rich in colour can cause clear braces or ceramic braces to stain and look unsightly. Once they are stained, it can be expensive and certainly inconvenient to replace the stained components. These foods can also cause elastic bands (if you have them) to stain too. This is not a huge problem as the bands are easier to replace, but it could cause them to look unsightly even if temporarily.

If you eat strongly coloured food, you will need to clean your teeth thoroughly immediately afterwards. However, even in doing so, you may find that some level of staining has already occurred.

Avoid Beetroot as they can cause staining

FOOD *for* BRACES

If you are concerned about staining and want to avoid this, then it is recommended that you avoid foods with strong colours such as blueberries, beetroot, anything containing turmeric such as yellow based curries, coffee, black tea, red wine, deeply coloured spices such as paprika and foods that have a thick and deeply coloured tomato- based sauce.

As a rule of thumb, if a food can stain a white shirt, it will probably stain your teeth.

Food for Braces

List of foods that stain braces

- Berries – Blueberries, Raspberries, Blackberries
- Yellow Curries
- Beetroot
- Black Coffee, tea (weak or herbal tea is ok)
- Red wine
- Rich tomato-based sauces
- Strongly pigmented spices such as turmeric and paprika

Avoid spices such as Tumeric

Your Handy Checklist of FOODS to Avoid while wearing BRACES

- Whole, raw, hard vegetables such as carrots

- Fruit that you take a big bite into or hard fruit e.g. whole apples (cut into thin slices instead)

- Crusty Bread and hard rolls

- Hard and crunchy croutons

- Bread with seeds and grains e.g. poppy seeds, sesame seeds and Multigrain Pizza crusts

- Corn on the cob – cut it off then eat it! Popcorn

- Nuts and dried fruit

- Tacos and Nachos – look for softer options

- Toffee or hard lollies

- Gummy lollies such as jubes, liquorice, snakes

- Hard biscuits

- Chewing Gum

- Hard chocolate and refrigerated chocolate

- Tough meats and eating meat off the bone e.g. chicken wings Beef jerky

- Muesli bars

Food for BRACES

Non-Food Things to avoid chewing on

- Avoid chewing the end of your pen or pen lid
- Do Not bite your fingernails!
- Ice Ice baby - do not crunch on ice!

Don't chew on the end of your pen!

FOOD for BRACES

Foods that are your Friend

Most of the time with braces, you will be able to eat relatively 'normal' food. Make life easy for yourself and aim to eat food that will not require too much chewing, and food that will not break your braces!

Meat and Protein

Great sources of easy to eat protein include chicken, tofu, beans, fish and eggs. Red meat is fine but needs to be tender and/or cut into small pieces.

Vegetables

Vegetables can be your friend and mashed potatoes is an all-time favourite, though most vegetables are ok as long as they are cooked until soft.

FOOD *for* BRACES

Fruit

Eating fruit is still ok, you just need to adapt a bit by cutting fruit into small bite size pieces or choose soft fruit such as bananas.

Carbohydrates

Pasta and soft bread are the best options. You can eat rice and other grains too, but you will find that cleaning your braces after eating small grains such as rice is a bit more effort.

FOOD *for* BRACES

Breakfast Ideas and Recipes

Apple Puree - perfect soft food

Ingredients:
- 2 Pink Lady or Granny Smith apples
- ½ tsp raw sugar (optional)
- Splash of water

Method:
1. Peel and core the apple, then finely chop.
2. Place chopped apple, sugar and a splash of water into a small pot on medium heat.
3. Cook for 5 minutes or until tender.
4. Use a fork to mash or a stick blender to puree.
5. Serve warm or cold.

Tip: make a big batch & freeze in portions and defrost one or two after each adjustment.

Food for BRACES

Banana and Cinnamon mash - fast and easy

Ingredients:
- 1 Banana
- Sprinkle of cinnamon

Method:
1. Peel and roughly chop banana into a bowl and mash with a fork.
2. Dust with cinnamon and enjoy.

Tip: this can also be used as the base for a simple smoothie, just add a cup of milk and whizz up in a blender.

Breakfast Smoothies!!!

About smoothies: these are a wonderful way to get a filling and nutritious meal or snack without the need to chew at all. Absolutely perfect for anytime when your teeth or gums are sore or just need a break.

Basic Ingredients:
- ¾ cup of your chosen milk – cow, almond, oat, rice
- 1 scoop of vanilla protein powder (optional)
- Add your choice of fruit

Method:
1. Add all ingredients to a blender and whizz!

Food for BRACES

Breakfast Smoothies!!! All the Colours of the RAINBOW!

- Strawberry smoothie – add ¼ cup strawberries for a pink delight that will please even the fussiest of eaters.
- Blueberry smoothie - add 1/3 cup blueberries. Blend thoroughly to avoid getting small pieces stuck in your braces.
- Banana smoothie – the ultimate filling smoothie! Add mashed banana with cinnamon or simply chop a whole banana into the smoothie and whiz it up.
- Mango and coconut - Add ½ mango and replace the milk with a small tin of coconut milk and water to make ¾ cup.
- Choccie - Add a spoonful of cocoa and half an avocado for a choccie hit that is packed with green goodness. Go on try it, it is yummier than it sounds! OR try a chocolate protein powder instead of the cocoa. This will mix beautifully with either strawberries or a banana.

Scrambled Eggs - a great protein source

Ingredients:
- 15g butter
- 6 eggs, lightly beaten
- 1/3 cup cooking cream

Method:
1. Crack the eggs into a mixing bowl and add the cream, salt and pepper and whisk until combined.
2. Melt the butter in a frying pan on a medium heat and swirl the melted butter to evenly coat the base of the pan.
3. Tip the egg mix into the pan and let it sit for 30 seconds, then gently fold the mixture from the outside in for a further 2 minutes.
4. Serve scrambled eggs on top of soft bread cut into soldiers.

Tip: Add 100g of chopped smoked salmon to the pan halfway thru cooking the eggs.

Food for BRACES

Tofu Scramble - great for vegetarians/vegans

This is a great alternative to scrambled eggs and is suitable for vegans.

Ingredients:
- 280g block of tofu
- ½ tsp smoked paprika
- 1 tsp ground cumin
- 1 tbsp olive oil
- Salt and pepper

Method:
1. Mash the tofu using a fork.
2. Heat the oil in a frypan and fry the mashed tofu on a medium heat for a few minutes.
3. Sprinkle with paprika and cumin and cook for a few more minutes, constantly stirring and lipping to ensure the tofu does not catch.
4. Season with salt & pepper. Serve with soft bread or a side of fresh chopped avocado.

Variation: Add finely diced, deseeded tomatoes & handful of mushrooms cut in small pieces.

FOOD for BRACES

Pancakes - a family favourite

Ingredients:
- 1 cup plain flour
- 2 tbsp caster sugar
- 1 egg
- ½ tsp vanilla essence
- 1 cup milk
- Canola oil for cooking Maple syrup (optional)

Method:
1. Sift flour into a bowl, add the sugar and mix.
2. Whisk ¾ cup milk, egg and vanilla together then add to the lour and mix well.
3. Add the remaining milk if needed to make a thick consistency.
4. Melt 1 tbsp butter in a frypan on medium heat and spread evenly.
5. Add a soup ladle of mixture to the pan.
6. When bubbles appear, lip using a spatula and cook the other side until lightly browned.
7. Serve with chopped banana or mango and a drizzle of maple syrup.

Serving Idea: Serve with chopped banana or mango and a drizzle of maple syrup.

Variation Idea: This recipe is for thinner style pancakes. If you want thicker pancakes, swap the plain flour for self-raising flour.

Pikelets - brilliant snacks and lunch box fillers

About this Recipe: these are one of the first things l learnt to cook by myself and have become a lifelong favourite. For many years l left the egg out to make egg-free and also substituted the milk for rice milk. They still turn out delicious but do burn easily so need to be watched carefully.

Ingredients:
- 1 ½ cups SR Flour
- 3 tbs raw sugar
- 1 egg
- 1 cup milk

Method:
1. Sift flour into a bowl, add the sugar and mix.
2. Whisk ¾ cup milk and the egg together then add to the flour and mix well.
3. Add the remaining milk if needed to make a thick consistency.
4. Melt 1 tbsp butter in a frypan on medium heat and spread evenly.
5. Add dessertspoons of mixture and watch as they start to bubble.
6. When bubbles appear, flip using a spatula and cook the other side until lightly browned.

Creamy Mushroom Open Sandwich - Yum!

Ingredients:
- 1 or 2 Slices of Sourdough (crusts removed) or any soft bread
- 100g mushrooms sliced
- 3 tbsp sour cream (optional) Salt and pepper
- 2 tbsp butter for cooking

Method"
1. Melt butter in a frypan on medium heat.
2. Add the mushrooms and move around the pan until lightly browned and soft.
3. If using sour cream, add to the pan and stir until just mixed.
4. Season with salt and pepper.
5. Serve immediately on a slice of soft bread with crusts removed.

Food for Braces

Muffins – the perfect brunch or lunchbox food

Muffins have always been a firm favourite in our house. Great for snacks, breakfast and such a great option for lunchboxes. For many years we have made ours without eggs and they turn out perfectly fine. In recent years we have started to add an egg and found that this does help them last a bit longer as they are not as dry. However, if you or anyone in your house is allergic to eggs, just leave the eggs out!

Pear and Dark Chocolate Muffins - crowd-pleaser!

Ingredients:
- 2 cups SR Flour
- ½ cup caster sugar
- ¼ cup melted butter
- 300ml milk (any type of milk can be used – cow's, almond, rice milk)
- 1 egg (optional)
- 2 x 120g store-bought diced pears in juice 150g Dark choc chips
- ½ tsp vanilla extract

Food for BRACES

Method:
1. Pre-heat the oven to 200 degrees Celsius and Line a muffin tray with patty pans.
2. Combine flour and sugar in a bowl.
3. Melt the butter in the microwave in 20 second bursts until just melted.
4. Make a well in the four and sugar mix.
5. Tip in the milk, butter and vanilla, mix lightly.
6. Whisk the egg in a small bowl and then add to the large bowl.
7. Mix lightly then add the pears and dark chocolate chips.
8. Mix until just combined and chunky ingredients are mixed in.
9. Bake for 15 to 20 minutes or until a skewer comes out clean when inserted into the middle of a muffin.

Variations:
- Apple and sultana muffins: swap the chopped pears and dark chocolate chips for chopped cooked apples and 100g sultanas (the sultanas will go soft).
- Double Chocolate: add 1.5 tablespoons of cocoa powder, leave out the fruit and add 50g white chocolate chips for a chocolate extravaganza!

Lunch and Dinner Recipes

This section starts off with light meals and moves on to more substantial recipes. The light meals are great for when your teeth and gums and sore and are also terrific side dishes to have with some of the substantial and meatier meals.

Mashed potatoes - your secret weapon

Mashed potatoes are your secret weapon! Why? Well, it is filling. It is non-acidic so perfect for when you have sore gums or ulcers. It is plain and so soft that you do not need to use your teeth at all. Best of all, even the fussiest of eaters likes potatoes! All these reasons make the humble mash one of your best go-to foods for sore teeth and sensitive gums.

Ingredients:

- 8 medium size white potatoes
- 2 tbsp of butter
- Salt and White Pepper

Method:
1. Peel and roughly chop the potatoes.
2. Add potatoes to a pot of boiling water. Bring to the boil, simmer for 10 minutes or until the potatoes are soft.
3. Take off the heat and drain.
4. Tip drained vegetable into a large bowl, add butter and mash until smooth.
5. Season with salt and white pepper.

Tips and Variation Ideas:
- Double/triple the quantities and freeze portions so you have a supply handy to use after each brace's adjustment.
- Make a quick gravy using a commercial gravy mix to make this a bit more of a simple meal for when you are sore.
- Pan fry thinly sliced mushrooms in butter & serve on top of the mash.
- Try adding sweet potato or chopped carrots to the boiling water and mash into the potatoes for an orange mash.

Cauliflower Cheese - a family favourite

Ingredients:
- 500g Cauliflower cut into florets
- 40g butter
- 500ml milk
- 1 tbsp cornflour
- 50g Cheddar grated
- 30g Parmesan grated
- White pepper

Method:
1. Boil or steam the cauliflower until tender then drain and put aside.
2. Melt the butter in a medium saucepan. When melted add the cornflour and mix well.
3. Gradually add the milk, stirring constantly to avoid lumps. Keep adding more milk, stir in, when mixed, add more milk.
4. Keep stirring the white sauce until sauce boils and thickens.
5. Add cheeses and mix until cheeses are melted in.
6. Season with white pepper.
7. Add the cauliflower into the sauce and gently fold in.

Guacamole – Good Old Smashed Avo!

Ingredients:
- 1 Avocado, halved, stone removed, fresh chopped and peeled
- ½ Tomato, seeds and pulp discarded, fresh finely chopped (optional)
- Salt and pepper

Method:
1. Place the chopped avocado in a bowl and mash with a fork.
2. Fold in diced tomato
3. Season with salt and pepper.
4. Serve on soft bread (with crust removed).

Tip: Most guacamole recipes use lime juice which I have omitted here as the acidity of the citrus can sting on sore gums.

Potato Salad – brilliant side dish or lunch box filler

Ingredients:
- 1kg White potatoes
- ½ cup mayonnaise
- ½ cup sour cream
- 1 tsp Dijon mustard
- 100g lunch meat – ham or turkey – cut into ribbons
- Herbs of choice (optional)

Method :
1. Peel and dice potatoes into 1 inch cubes.
2. Boil a large pot of salted water.
3. Add potatoes and cook for 10 minutes or until potatoes are just cooked.
4. Strain potatoes in a colander and allow to cool.
5. Mix mayo, sour cream and mustard then season with salt and pepper.
6. Toss the creamy mix with the potatoes and meat in a large bowl.
7. Add herbs such as finely chopped parsley or chives but note that these will probably get stuck in your braces, so it might be best to leave them out.

Lettuce and Blue Cheese salad - tasty lunch or side dish

Ingredients:
- ¼ Iceberg lettuce, shredded
- 1 eating apple cut into matchsticks
- 8 thin slices of cucumber cut into quarters
- 20g Blue Cheese
- Honey to drizzle

Method:
1. Shred the lettuce and chop the cucumber and apple into thin slices or matchsticks.
2. Place the lettuce in a bowl, top with the apple and cucumber, and crumble the blue cheese over the top.
3. Drizzle with honey then serve.

Ideas:
- If you don't like blue cheese, substitute with your cheese of choice, just be sure to avoid hard cheeses.
- Top with any herbs you may have on hand. Chives or dill would be lovely. You can also put this combination in a wrap and add mayo.
- Add a small tin of tuna or salmon and turn into a substantial meal.

Food for Braces

Fish Patties - simply delicious

Ingredients:
- 750g raw white fish fillets
- ¼ breadcrumbs
- ½ brown onion grated
- 1 tsp lemon zest
- ¼ cup dill or parsley finely chopped
- 1 egg*
- Salt and pepper
- Vegetable oil for cooking

Method:

1. Roughly chop fish and put into a food processor. Pulse until chopped, be careful not to overwork the fish or it will turn into a paste.
2. Put fish, breadcrumbs, onion, lemon zest, herbs and egg in a bowl and mix together.
3. Season well with salt and pepper.
4. Add a tablespoon of oil to a frypan on a moderate heat.
5. Use a tablespoon to scoop the fish mixture and add to the pan, pressing the fish cake gently with the back of the spoon to even out.
6. Cook for a couple of minutes on each side.
7. Repeat in batches until all mixture has been used.
8. Eat on their own with mayo or tartare sauce or make it a more substantial meal by serving with mashed potatoes.

Variation Idea:

To make this egg free, add 2 tablespoons of plain flour. This will help bind the mixture. Swap the white fish for two 415g tins of Red or Pink Salmon. Instead of step 1 above, do this: Open the tins, drain and remove excess skin and bones. Then use your hands to lake the salmon into the mixing bowl and mix together with the other ingredients.

Food for Braces

Potato and Leek Soup - smooth and satisfying

This is the perfect first week meal. Everyone loves potatoes and it is a quite easy soup to make. Best of all, it will please even the fussiest of eaters.

Ingredients:
- 8 medium size white potatoes
- 1 Leek thinly sliced
- 1 litre Chicken Stock
- 1 tbsp Olive Oil
- 2 tbsp Cooking Cream (optional)
- Salt and White Pepper

Method:
1. Thinly sliced the white part of the leek.
2. Heat the olive oil in a large pot then add the leek and cook until soft but not brown.
3. Peel and roughly chop the potatoes then add to the pan along with the chicken stock.
4. Bring to the boil then simmer for 15 minutes or until the potatoes are soft.
5. Take off the heat and use a stab mixer to puree until smooth.
6. Add the cream and add small amounts of water to thin out soup if necessary.
7. Season with salt and white pepper.

Serving Idea:

Serve with soft white bread (no seeds!) such as Brioche– or - use any non-seeded bread, cut the hard crusts off (use these to make breadcrumbs and freeze), and cut into small cubes and sprinkle on top of the soup. The fresh bread 'croutons will soak up the soup and be nice and soft to eat. This will help make the soup feel more filling.

Fish Chowder - so tasty!

Ingredients:
- 50g butter
- 1 leek finely sliced
- 1 carrot diced into 1cm cubes
- 1 celery stalk finely chopped
- 2 potatoes, peeled and diced into 1 cm pieces
- 1 tbsp cornflour
- 3 cups fish or chicken stock
- 500 g white fish fillet chopped
- ½ cup cream
- Salt and pepper

Method:
1. Melt a tablespoon of the butter then add the leek, carrot, celery and potatoes.
2. Cook over a moderate heat, stirring to prevent the vegetables catching on the pan, until
3. the carrot has just softened. Don't worry if the potatoes are not cooked thru at this stage.
4. Push the vegetables to one side of the pan and add the remaining butter. When melted add the cornflour and mix to make a roux.
5. Add the stock one ladle full at a time and vigourously mix with the roux to ensure no lumps. Keep adding the remaining stock and mix with the vegetables.
6. Bring to the boil, then lower the heat and simmer for a few minutes. The potatoes should now be soft, and the mixture has slightly thickened.
7. Using a stab mixer, puree half of the soup so that it is half chunky and half pureed.
8. Add the fish and cook for a few more minutes until it is cooked thru.
9. If you would prefer a smoother chowder, use the stab mixer again and puree your soup to the desired consistency.
10. Add the cream, heat thru without bringing to the boil.
11. If the soup is a little thick, add soup ladles of stock one at a time and mix until the desired consistency is reached.
12. Season with salt and pepper and your soup is ready.

Serving Idea:
Serve with some soft brioche or chop up any type of bread into cubes and place on top to soften and help fill you up!

Corn Chowder - great comfort food

Ingredients:
- 50g butter
- 1 onion finely sliced
- 1 carrot diced into 1cm cubes
- 1 celery stalk finely chopped
- 1 potato, peeled and diced into 1 cm pieces
- 3 cups fish, vegetable or chicken stock 500g frozen corn kernels
- ½ cup cream
- Salt and pepper

Method:
1. Melt a tablespoon of the butter then add the onion, carrot, celery and potato.
2. Cook over a moderate heat, stirring to prevent the vegetables catching on the pan, until the vegetables have softened and lightly browned.
3. Add the stock and corn kernels and bring to the boil, then lower the heat and simmer for a few minutes.
4. Add the cream, heat thru without bringing to the boil.
5. Using a stab mixer, puree the soup. Puree until completely smooth so there are no little bits to get trapped in your braces.
6. If the soup is a little thick, add additional ladles of stock until the desired consistency is reached.
7. Season with salt and pepper and your soup is ready.

Serving Idea:
Serve with some soft brioche or chop up any type of bread into cubes and place on top to soften and help fill you up!

Food for BRACES

Chicken Noodle Soup - Soul food!

Ingredients:
- 2 tbsp olive oil
- 1 brown onion, finely chopped
- 1 medium carrot, peeled and sliced thinly
- 1 stick celery, finely diced
- 1 medium potato, peeled and diced into 1cm pieces
- 3 cups chicken stock
- 1 store-bought BBQ chicken or 250g (approx.) chicken breast fillet
- 100g rice noodles or small pasta shapes
- 1/2 tsp mild curry powder

Method:
1. Heat oil in pan, add curry powder (it is only a small amount but makes a big difference), onion, carrot, celery and potato and cook for 5 to 8 minutes or until vegetables have softened.
2. Add the chicken stock and bring to the boil before reducing heat and simmering for 5 minutes.
3. Remove the breast meat from the chicken and chop into 1cm pieces. Alternately, chop the raw chicken fillet and add to the pan.
4. Use scissors to cut the rice noodles into approximately 1 inch size lengths and add to the pan.
5. Bring to the boil then reduce heat and simmer for 5 to 10 minutes or until the noodles have softened and if using raw meat, that the chicken has cooked thru.
6. Season with salt and pepper and serve with soft bread.

Baked Salmon with steamed vegies

Ingredients:
- 4 x skin-free Salmon fillets (or one for each person)
- 2 lemons sliced
- Salt and pepper
- Bunch of asparagus (or any greens you prefer)
- 5 white potatoes peeled and cut into 2 inch pieces
- 1 tbsp olive oil
- 1 tbsp butter

Method:
1. Preheat the oven to 200 degrees Celsius.
2. Grease an oven tray and lay the lemon slices out to make a bed.
3. Season the salmon fillets with sea salt, black pepper and olive oil.
4. Place the salmon fillets on top of the lemon and put in the oven to bake for 12 minutes or until done.
5. Boil the potatoes until tender, then toss with the butter.
6. Boil, steam or pan-fry the asparagus.
7. Serve the salmon with potatoes and asparagus.

Tip: This is equally delicious with any type of white fish and you can swap oven baking for pan-frying.

Creamy Salmon and Pea Pasta - a taste sensation!

Ingredients:
- 300g macaroni
- 3 tbsp butter
- 1 brown onion, finely diced
- 1 celery stalk, finely diced
- 1 large carrot finely diced
- 2 tbsp cornflour
- 3 cups milk
- 400g raw salmon fillet chopped into 2cm dice or 2 fillets cooked salmon
- 1 cup frozen peas
- 1/3 cup grated parmesan cheese

Method:
1. Cook macaroni according to packet directions, drain and put to the side (drizzle with a little olive oil to stop it sticking together).
2. Microwave the peas according to packet directions.
3. Melt 1 tbsp butter in pan and add onion, celery and carrots and stir until softened.
4. Push to one side, add the remaining butter and melt.
5. Add cornflour to the melted butter to make a roux.
6. Gradually add milk, stirring constantly to avoid lumps and start mixing with the vegetables.
7. Once all the milk is added, bring to the boil then reduce heat. Add raw salmon (if using) and cook for 5 minutes. If using hot smoked salmon, add at the end of the 5 minutes.
8. Drain the peas. Add the peas, parmesan and macaroni to the pan and gently combine.
9. Season with pepper and you are ready to serve.

FOOD for BRACES

Chicken and Noodle Stir-fry

Ingredients:
- 500g chicken mince or chicken thighs cut into small pieces
- 400g noodles – any type of noodles: egg noodles, rice noodles, udon noodles
- 1 carrot cut into sticks
- ½ red capsicum cut into sticks
- ½ cup shredded green cabbage
- 100g bean sprouts
- 2 tbsp Oyster sauce
- 2 tbsp Soy sauce
- 1 tsp pureed ginger (store-bought)

Method:
1. Prepare your chosen noodles as per packet directions and put to one side while preparing everything else.
2. Heat 1 tbsp oil in a wok on high heat.
3. Add the chicken, ginger and tablespoon of soy sauce and stir-fry until the chicken is cooked.
4. Add the carrot, capsicum and cabbage and stir-fry for a few minutes.
5. Add the oyster sauce and remaining tablespoon of soy sauce and stir quickly.
6. Add the bean sprouts and noodles and toss until the noodles are coated in sauce (add a couple of splashes of water if needed).

Variations:
- Add Eggs - After adding the noodles and mixing for a minute, push all ingredients to one side of the wok, then add two whisked eggs to the pan and keep scrambling. When cooked thru, fold the noodle mixture back over the top and mix the eggs thru.
- Any type of meat can be used in this recipe. Substitute the chicken for beef, or even add shrimps.

Meatloaf - great as tasty leftovers in lunchboxes!

Ingredients:
- 500g Pork mince
- 1 grated carrot
- 1 minced or grated onion 50g breadcrumbs
- 30g feta cheese
- 1 tablespoon chopped fresh oregano or 1stp dried oregano Sea salt and white pepper
- Olive oil

Method:
1. Pre-heat the oven to 200 degrees Celsius.
2. Add the mince, carrot, onion, herbs and breadcrumbs to a bowl.
3. Crumbled in the feta and mix with your hands.
4. Season with salt and pepper.
5. Line a baking tray with baking paper, shape the mixture in a log and place on tray.
6. Drizzle with olive oil, then place in the oven to cook for 20 to 25 minutes or until lightly browned and cooked in the centre.
7. Serve slices of meatloaf with gravy, mashed potatoes or boiled/steamed soft vegetables of your choice.

Tip: Use leftover meatloaf slices as lunch box snacks or for sandwich fillings.

Savoury Mince - a hearty winter warmer

This is a great alternative to Spaghetti Bolognese. Spag Bog has a rich tomato sauce that can cause staining issues. We have all seen small children with red staining around their mouths after eating spag bog. Likewise, it can have this effect on your braces, especially if you have ceramic braces. The recipe below still uses mince so it is easy to eat, but without the staining issues. Best of all it is nice and tasty.

Ingredients:
- 500g mince – beef, pork or chicken
- ½ cup frozen peas
- 1 medium brown onion, finely chopped
- ½ medium carrot, grated or diced
- 1 garlic clove, grated (optional)
- 1 tbsp cornflour
- 1 beef or chicken stock cube
- 1 tbsp Worcestershire sauce
- 1 tbsp olive oil

Method:
1. Heat oil in a pan over moderate heat.
2. Add carrots and cook for a few minutes before adding the onion and garlic and cook for a further few minutes.
3. Follow the instructions on the packet of peas to cook. My favourite method is to microwave them.
4. Add the mince and break the mince into smaller pieces while stirring.
5. Fill the kettle with water and put on the boil.
6. When the mince has cooked thru and is no longer pink, crumble in the stock cube and add a cup of boiling water from the kettle.
7. Bring to the boil and then reduce to simmer for 10 minutes.
8. Mix the cornflour with 2 tablespoons of water until smooth then add to the mince and stir until thickened.
9. Season with salt and pepper.
10. Add the Worcestershire sauce and peas, stir in for a minute before turning the heat off.

Cottage Pie – classic comfort food

Ingredients:
- 1 x Savoury Mince recipe
- 1 x Mashed Potato recipe
- 1 tablespoon grate parmesan

Method:
1. Preheat oven to 200 degrees Celsius.
2. Grease a casserole or baking dish.
3. Prepare the mince and mashed potatoes as per the recipes elsewhere in this book.
4. Spread the mince evenly in the prepared baking dish, then top with the mashed potatoes.
5. Draw lines on the top of the mashed potatoes with the back of a fork.
6. Sprinkle lightly with parmesan.

Tip: This is also delicious with sweet potato mash mixed with white potatoes.

Food for Braces

Pulled Pork – a Slow Cooker Favourite

Ingredients:
- 1.5kg Pork shoulder
- 1 brown onion
- 2 tbsp brown sugar
- 1 tbsp ground cumin
- 1 tbsp smoked paprika
- 1 tsp garlic powder
- Salt and pepper
- 100ml chicken stock
- 100ml tangy BBQ sauce (store-bought)

FOOD *for* BRACES

Method:
1. Slice onions and pan-fry lightly until cooked thru but only slightly browned. Remove and set aside.
2. Combine sugar, cumin, paprika, garlic powder and a good grinding of salt and pepper in a bowl.
3. Rub spice mix onto pork shoulder.
4. Pan-fry pork shoulder and brown all over.
5. Add onions to the slow cooker and place pork on top.
6. Add stock, then the BBQ sauce.
7. Put slow cooker on for six hours on low setting.
8. When ready, remove the pork and shred the tender pork using two forks.
9. Add the pork back into the slow cooker and toss with the onions and sauce. Add more BBQ sauce if required.
10. Serve with mashed potatoes and green peas.

Roasted Sweet Potato, Feta and Basil Pasta Salad

Pasta salads are great for lunch, dinner and for packed lunches too!

Ingredients
- 500g Sweet Potato, peeled and chopped into 2cm cubes
- 250g pasta spirals (or any pasta you have on hand!)
- 100g Feta cheese
- 20g Basil leaves, shredded
- Olive oil, sea salt and cracked pepper

Avocado Dressing:
- 1 ripe avocado, chopped
- 1 tbsp fresh lemon juice (optional)
- 2 tbsp extra virgin olive oil
- Salt and pepper

Method:
1. Preheat the oven to 200C & line a large baking tray with baking paper.
2. Scatter the chopped sweet potato on the tray, drizzle with oil, season with salt and pepper and toss with your hands until coated.
3. Roast for 20 minutes, or until lightly browned then remove from the oven and allow to cool.
4. Cook the pasta by following the packet directions.
5. Drain the pasta and rinse with cold water.
6. For the dressing, simply combine all ingredients in a blender or food processor and process until smooth.
7. Gently mix the pasta, roasted sweet potato and dressing until combined.
8. Sprinkle with crumbled feta and shredded basil.

Serving Suggestion:
Add cooked chopped chicken and kalamata olives for a Mediterranean feast.

Food for Braces

Bocconcini and fresh tomato pasta salad

Ingredients:
- 300g Farfalle or Shell Pasta 220g Bocconcini (baby sized)
- 200g cherry tomatoes chopped in half or quarters 200g Spinach leaves
- ¼ red onion, finely sliced (optional)
- Honey Mustard Dressing
- 1 tbsp honey
- 1 tbsp extra virgin olive oil
- 1 tbsp white wine vinegar
- 1 tsp Dijon mustard
- Salt and pepper

Method:
1. Cook the pasta according to packet directions. Drain and allow to cool.
2. Add bocconcini, tomatoes, spinach, onion and pasta to a large bowl and loosely toss to combine.
3. Add all dressing ingredients to a small bowl and whisk to combine. Season with salt and pepper.
4. Add dressing to pasta bowl and toss to combine.

Food for BRACES

DESSERT Recipes

Cottage cheese and chopped fruit – fast and easy

Ingredients:
- 100g Cottage Cheese
- Small handful of strawberries or your chosen fruit
- Cinnamon
- Caster sugar (optional) or Splenda (sugar alternative)

Method:
1. Spoon the ricotta into a bowl and top with chopped fruit.
2. Sprinkle with cinnamon and sugar and you are ready to eat!

FOOD for BRACES

Stewed Fruit – great for dessert or breakfast

Ingredients:
- ½ cup water
- ½ cup caster sugar
- ½ tsp vanilla bean paste
- 1 cinnamon stick
- 250g strawberries or pears or apricots

Method:
1. Add the water and sugar to a saucepan and heat until the sugar dissolves.
2. Add the vanilla and cinnamon stick, bring to the boil and simmer for 3 minutes.
3. Add your choice of fruit and cook on low heat for 3 to 5 minutes.
4. Remove the cinnamon stick.
5. Serve the fruit hot or cold.

Serving Ideas:
- Add a spoonful or two to the top of your breakfast porridge.
- Serve with ice cream, cream or custard for a delicious dessert.

Food for BRACES

Smooth Banana Dessert Bowl - a sweet delight

Ingredients:
- 1 Banana
- 1/2 cup milk*
- 2 scoops vanilla ice-cream*
- 1 tbsp honey
- Drizzle of vanilla extract

Method:
1. Put all the ingredients in a blender and whizz it up until smooth. So easy!

Tip: make this dairy free by using soy/almond/rice milk and replace the ice-cream with soy ice-cream.

Soft Cookies – cookie treats that won't break braces!

These cookies are perfect to eat with ice cream for dessert, or pack and go as your perfect lunch box filler or snack on the run.

The secret to making cookies soft is adding milk and using mixed flours. Most cookies have the basic ingredients of flour, sugar and butter. The butter is effectively what makes them crunchy when baked. By adding milk (which is not usually found in cookies) and SR flour, we are softening the mixture and almost making a stiff cake mixture.

Ingredients:
- 1 cup plain flour
- 1 cup SR flour
- ½ cup butter
- 1 egg
- 1/3 cup caster sugar
- 100g Choc Chips (optional)

Method :
1. Preheat oven to 180 degrees Celsius and line a tray with baking paper.
2. Sift plain flour, SR flour and sugar together.
3. Microwave the butter until soft but not melted.
4. Whisk the milk, egg and butter together, then add to the dry ingredients and mix.
5. Add the choc chips (if using) and mix thru until evenly distributed.
6. Use a tablespoon to portion mixture, shape into a ball then flatten between your two palms until 1cm thick and place on baking tray, 2cm apart.
7. Bake for 14 minutes

Apple Crumble - great for all the family to enjoy

Ingredients:
- 6 to 8 Apples
- 1/3 cup raw sugar 1/3 cup water

Crumble:
- ½ cup Self-Raising flour 80g butter
- ¼ cup raw sugar
- Sprinkle of cinnamon

Food for Braces

Method:
1. Peel apples, slice off flesh leaving the core. Dice the apple chunks.
2. Add water, sugar and diced apples to a saucepan and bring to the boil, then simmer until apples are soft.
3. To make the crumble, melt the butter in the microwave.
4. Mix flour, butter and sugar in a bowl.
5. Tip apples into a baking dish.
6. Crumble the flour mix evenly over the top of the apples.
7. Sprinkle cinnamon over the top.
8. Bake in oven at 180C for 20 min or until brown on top.

Tip: This is a super easy recipe. Make sure you have a couple of peelers handy, put the music on and have fun making this one together with family and friends.

Serving Idea: Drizzle with runny custard and a scoop of vanilla ice-cream…yum!

Self-Saucing Chocolate Pudding – chocolate heaven

Ingredients:
- 2 cups SR Flour
- ½ cup caster sugar
- ¼ Cocoa
- ¼ cup melted butter
- 150ml milk
- 1 egg (optional)
- Canola oil for greasing

Sauce Ingredients:
- ¾ cup firmly packed brown sugar
- 2 tbsp cocoa
- 1 ½ cups boiling water

Food for Braces

Method
1. Preheat the oven to 180 degrees Celsius.
2. Grease an oven-proof casserole dish lightly with oil.
3. Combine dry ingredients in a bowl.
4. Combine milk and egg and whisk together with melted butter (after it has cooled or it will cook the egg).
5. Add wet ingredients to the dry ingredients and mix well.
6. Tip into the prepared dish.
7. To make the chocolate sauce, mix the cocoa and sugar in a bowl. Add the boiling water gradually, mixing to avoid lumps.
8. Gently pour the sauce over the batter.
9. Put in the oven to bake for 30 minutes. The cake will have risen to the top and the sauce will be at the bottom.
10. Serve hot with ice cream or cream. Simply delicious.

FOOD *for* BRACES

Apple Pudding - You will be going back for seconds!

Ingredients:
- 6 to 8 green apples
- 2 tbsp caster sugar
- 1/3 cup water

Cake topping:
- ½ cup Self-Raising flour
- 1 cup milk
- 1 egg
- 2 level tbsp butter melted
- ¼ cup caster sugar
- ½ tsp vanilla extract

Food for Braces

Method:
1. Peel apples and cut into slices.
2. Add water, sugar and apples to a saucepan, bring to the boil, then simmer until apples are soft.
3. Mix milk, egg, vanilla and sugar in a bowl.
4. Add the melted butter after it has cooled.
5. Sift in the lour and mix.
6. Place apples into a baking dish.
7. Pour over the cake batter.
8. Bake in oven at 180C for 20 min or until lightly browned on top.

Idea: Substitute pears for the apples.

Pear Clafoutis - sophisticated and delicious

Fruit
- 5 pears, peeled, cored and cut into quarters and halved again (into eights!)
- 1 tbsp caster sugar
- 1 vanilla bean pod
- 1 cup water

Batter Ingredients
- 1/3 cup SR flour
- 2 eggs
- ¼ cup sugar
- 1 cup milk
- ½ teaspoon vanilla extract
- Butter for greasing the baking dish
- 1 tbsp Icing sugar for dusting

FOOD for BRACES

Method:
1. Preheat the oven to 180 degrees Celsius.
2. Scrape out a vanilla bean pod and add the paste to a pot with the water and pears. Cook until the pears are soft, turning occasionally and adding small amounts of hot water if needed. Once cooked, allow the pears to cool.
3. Mix the flour, sugar, eggs and milk together, then use a cake mixer to mix until smooth (no lumps!).
4. Grease a 20cm baking dish with melted butter.
5. Arrange the pears evenly in the dish.
6. Pour over the batter and place in the over to cook for 30 minutes or until a skewer comes out clean.
7. Dust the top with icing sugar and serve with cream or ice-cream.

EASY Lunchbox Solutions

Packing a lunchbox to take to school, work or for travelling needs to consider temperature requirements. If you are taking dairy products or any food that needs to be kept at the correct temperature, you may need to pack an insulated container and/or cold packs. Some easy ideas:

- Chopped soft fruit – banana, melon, seedless grapes, kiwi fruit
- Cottage cheese mixed with diced strawberries and cinnamon
- Hummus (or other dip) with soft pita bread for dipping
- Yoghurt
- Pureed or diced fruit cups (store-bought or make your own)
- Muffins or cupcakes
- Slices of baked ricotta
- Thinly sliced lunch meats such as ham, polony/spam, turkey and potato salad
- Leftover pasta or pasta salad

Food for BRACES

Sandwiches

Use a soft style of bread and cut off the crusts. Go one step further and cut your sandwiches into smaller portions (triangles, tin soldiers or bite sized pieces) so your teeth don't have to work too hard.

Use fillings such as thinly sliced cold meats such as ham (avoid chewy meat such as prosciutto or salami), polony, turkey, leftover meatloaf, thinly sliced cheese or grated cheese and tomato, tuna and mayo, creamed cheese.

Use your dinner leftovers

Lunch box ideas other than sandwiches are plentiful. In my opinion, the best lunch is always last night's leftovers! If you have access to a microwave, some of these options can be reheated for a hot lunch. Dinner leftovers could be any of the following:
- Soup
- Slow-cooked or stewed tender meat and vegetables
- Potato salad
- Pasta – if it was hot the night before, eat it cold and call it a salad!
- Fried Rice or Risotto

Food for BRACES

Tips for Eating Out AND Ordering Take-away

Going out for Breakfast or Brunch

Foods to Avoid:
- Breakfast burgers Bagels
- Toasted sandwiches
- Fried chicken (yes, some people eat this for brekkie!) Crusty toast or bread with hard crusts

Breakfast and Brunch are full of great options.

Consider these great ideas:
- Scrambled Eggs
- Eggs Benedict
- Bacon is ok as long as it is not too crispy
- Pancakes and waffles
- Banana Bread
- Bircher Muesli (no nuts or dried fruit)
- Smashed avocado on toast (cut off the hard crusts before eating)
- Muffins (no nuts and avoid staining berries such as blueberries) Iced chocolate
- Coffee diluted with milk
- Fresh juices

Japanese Food - tasty but can be sticky

Sushi is yummy but the sticky rice can be a nuisance to pick out of your braces. Only eat sushi if you are able to thoroughly pick and clean your braces immediately afterwards. Go soft fillings such as avocado or omelette.

Foods to Avoid:
- Crispy deep-fried food
- Curry

Better Food Choices:
- Sashimi (raw fish - avoid squid)
- Teriyaki fish or chicken (chop into bite-size pieces) Miso soup
- Tamagyoki - Japanese omelette
- Udon noodles
- Ramen

Burger Joints - avoid braces busters!

Burgers are big bite food. The action of taking a big bite of a burger can damage your braces.

Burgers at home can be eaten using a knife and fork to cut the burger into small bite sized pieces. However, if you are out at a burger joint this might not be the best option.

Instead think about ordering potatoes wedges and avoid the crispy ones!

Pizza - Eating out and Take-away

Avoid Hard Crusts on Pizza as these will break your braces.. Cut the crust off the pizza and use a knife and fork to cut your pizza into bite size portions so you are not damaging your braces by taking big bites.

Also consider ordering a white-based pizzas that does not have the traditional tomato base, as the tomato base can cause staining of your braces and teeth. Remember to brush your teeth after eating rich-coloured food to avoid staining.

Italian Food - creamy pastas are perfect

Avoid rich tomato-based pastas, these can stain your teeth and braces. Have you ever seen a toddler in a highchair after eating spaghetti with tomato smeared all over their face?

Even after wiping a baby's face the tomato leaves a slight stain. Imagine this on your teeth/braces.

Go for creamy pasta options instead which are soft and easy to eat and will not stain your braces and teeth.

Filled pasta such as ravioli or tortellini are also good options.

Garlic bread is fine, just chop off the crispy crusts.

FOOD for BRACES

Chinese Food - lots of great options

Some judgement is required with Chinese food due to the large and varied menu of food on offer. Avoid crispy fried food and nuts (sometimes included in stir-fry dishes).

Apart from that, Chinese food offers some great options as much of the food is already cut into bite-size pieces. Some easy options include:
- Chow Mein (with soft noodles not crispy)
- Omelette
- Fried Rice
- Steamed dumplings
- Scallops, prawns, chicken off the bone, fish (no bones)
- Stir-fry's
- Noodles

Food for BRACES

Indian Food can be tricky

Most Indian food is rich in colour and flavour. Unfortunately, this is a problem due to potential staining issues. You will need avoid any dishes containing turmeric, rich tomato curries and tandoori. My advice is to avoid it for a while, you won't be wearing braces for ever. If you simply must eat a curry, clean your teeth thoroughly straight away afterwards.
A few safe (albeit limited) options include:
- Raita (yoghurt)
- Steamed rice
- Garlic prawns
- Onion bhaji (cut into bite-size pieces)
- Creamy cardamon based curries (no tumeric)
- Naan bread, chapati, paratha
- Mango lassi
- Gulab Jamun (sweet dumplings)

Thai Food - some great tasty options

Avoid strong spices, crispy fried food, curries and satay dishes (which contains nuts). There are lots of great choices with Thai food! Consider these:

- Egg noodles, rice noodles, Pad Thai (noodles) – ask for your noodles without nuts.
- Stir-fries
- Pad Kra Pao Moo or Laab Moo - Minced pork
- Wonton Soup, Coconut soup, Tom Yum (spicy - avoid if you have sore gums)
- Fried Rice
- Omelette
- Steamed Fish and Fish Cakes

Food for Braces

American Food - avoid big bites!

Eating classic American food can be problematic as a lot of it is 'big bite' food which will break your braces. The following should be avoided:
- Ribs - avoid completely
- Hot Dogs
- Buffalo Wings
- Fried Chicken
- Reuben Sandwich

Better choices include:
- Burgers can be eaten with care. Do not take big bites. Cut into small pieces irst.
- Meatloaf and spam
- Tub of mashed potato and gravy
- Chips/Fries - avoid hard, crisp ones Chicken nuggets
- Cornbread
- Macaroni and cheese
- New York Cheesecake

Fast Food - What to Eat and What to Avoid

Food to avoid:
- Hot Dogs
- Burgers (unless you can eat with a knife and fork)
- Crispy tacos
- Kebabs
- Pizza Crust
- Fried Chicken

Better Choices:
- Chips – avoid crisp ones
- Burgers eaten by chopping into small bite-sized pieces (yes I know this is in both lists!) Fish and Chips
- Chicken nuggets - cut or break into small bite-size pieces
- Tub of mashed potato and gravy
- Pizza - cut into pieces and avoid the crunchy crust

Food for BRACES

Eating Out and Choosing Desserts

Avoid biting into churros and pretzels

The good news is there are plenty of yummy options, such as:
- Ice cream and Gelato - avoid crispy cones and ask for yours in a cup
- Sundaes without nuts
- Trifle
- Donuts – break into small pieces
- Chocolate brownie (no nuts)
- Fruit salad - soft fruits (no raspberries or blueberries which can cause staining)

Can I Eat that? Your Frequently Asked Questions about eating with braces answered!

When researching for this book, I looked at some common Google searches related to 'Food for Braces.' Outlined below are some commonly googled questions. Perhaps these are questions you may have at some point too?

Keep your eye open for the one question that I found surprising!! Can you spot it?

Food for BRACES

Can you eat popcorn with braces?

No! Absolutely not. When a popcorn kernel pops, the outer shell of the seed forms part of the popcorn. This is the hull and this part of the popcorn is thin, sharp and lat. If these get stuck in your braces, they can be incredibly difficult to remove.

If you are looking for something savoury to eat at the cinema, opt for potato crisps instead.

Can you eat chips with braces?

There are two types of chips – hot chips (fries) and potato crisps. Both of these are ok to eat. I can almost hear the sigh of relief. Chips are life for some people. Hot chips can be great for those with a poor appetite or those reluctant to eat. Who can resist a hot chip? Be sure that the hot chips are not overly crunchy and enjoy.

Food for BRACES

Can you eat chocolate with braces?

Yes, but not all chocolate. Avoid chocolate containing nuts or other hard crunchy things like Smarties or M&M's and avoid refrigerated chocolate which will make the chocolate hard. Chocolates with praline fillings or soft centres are suitable.

Can you eat ice cream with braces?

Yes. Yes. Yes. Ice cream is perfect because you can eat it without needing to chew. This makes ice cream a great snack for when you have sore teeth and gums.

What candy / lollies can you eat with braces?

Yes, you can eat some candy/lollies with braces. Jelly type lollies such as snakes and jelly babies will be sticky and make a horrible mess of your braces and are best avoided.
Don't even think about toffee, caramel or liquorice.
Easier options are soft chocolates, Kit Kats, Marshmallows or head to the biscuit aisle at the supermarket to find chocolate biscuits that are not too hard to bite into.

Can you eat cereal with braces?

Eating cereal is a minefield with braces. Avoid hard crunchy cereals and avoid cereals with dried fruits and nuts. Hot cereals are often the best option as the cereal is softened in the cooking process. Porridge is a perfect example. Another alternative is home-made Bircher muesli (without nuts and without dried fruit) which is soaked overnight to soften the cereal.

Can you drink coffee with braces?

Yes and No. Avoid strong black coffee. Instead opt for coffee with milk.

After drinking any type of coffee, rinse your mouth out, brush your teeth afterwards to help prevent staining.

Can you eat marshmallows with braces?

Marshmallows are nice and soft so should be ok. However, they are very, very high in sugar so you will need to clean your teeth afterwards.

Can you eat peanut butter and/or jam/jelly with braces?

It's still possible to enjoy classics such as a peanut butter and jelly sandwich while wearing braces. Chunky peanut butter should be avoided altogether, but creamy peanut butter is usually fine. Just remember to brush your teeth as soon as possible to remove all peanut butter from the brackets.

Can you eat rice with braces?

Yes, rice is fine to eat with braces. Steamed rice is a great bland food option if you are looking for something filling for when you have sensitive gums. It can be a bit of a clean-up task afterwards though as the rice can get stuck in your braces.

Can you eat bread with braces?

Yes and no. Soft bread such as brioche and soft loaves with the crusts removed are ok. Bread with seeds should be avoided and hard crusts should always be avoided.

FOOD *for* BRACES

Can you eat goldfish with braces?

THIS is the surprising question I discovered that people apparently ask of Google!!!

Of course, the answer is NO. I do not recommend eating a goldfish under any circumstances because they are too cute!
However, if you need further convincing (?!), then it is not recommended due to the small bones that will potentially damage your braces.

Food *for* BRACES

Tempting Fussy Eaters

I have always had a belief that mealtimes should be harmonious and not a battle ground. Many families have battles with getting children to eat greens and healthy foods. I have been in that space too and that is without adding braces into the mix.

In the first few weeks (or even longer) of getting braces, the person with braces may be even fussier than they were before. This is perfectly understandable and there are plenty of ways to tempt a fussy eater. I have included some ideas below because I have seen and heard so many stories about dinner time battles over the years. I have often given out advice that has been welcomed by frustrated parents. Not every idea will work, but I can guarantee that fighting at the dinner table and forcing kids to eat with threats of 'no dessert' or 'no internet' if they don't eat all their vegetables, is a doomed approach.

FOOD *for* BRACES

9 Winning Ideas for tempting fussy eaters

1. Give them ownership. Let kids help decide what to buy, what to cook and what is for dinner that night.
2. Let them help at the shops. Go to the fruit and vegetable section and let them choose any 2 or 3 items of their choice.
3. If you are feeling confident with their fruit and vegetable selection, you can take this a step further next time and ask them to pick any 2 green vegetables. If they need to be bribed, offer to buy a small treat to have after dinner too. Again, let them choose the treat (as long it is not on the food to avoid list!). By letting them choose the greens and the treat, they have made an agreement with you. Make sure you deliver on the promise but don't use it as threat.

Food for BRACES

4. Let them pick a recipe from a family-friendly cookbook and either cook it together or if they want to cook themselves, let them go for it.
5. Eat at the dinner table, put all food in the middle, and allow central serving. Each person only puts on their plate what they want to eat. Children are encouraged to eat vegetables, even if it is only a small amount. If they refuse, just ignore.
6. Dinner time is positive vibes only. No-one is allowed to call something yucky, gross or say, 'I hate that.' If you don't like it, push it quietly to the side. If a person has gone to the trouble to cook food, they deserve the food to be respected. Explain the rules calmly and remind them when needed.
7. No-one is allowed to say 'I don't like it' if they have never tried it. If they try it (at least a couple of times) and still don't like it, then fair enough. We all have aversions to some food.

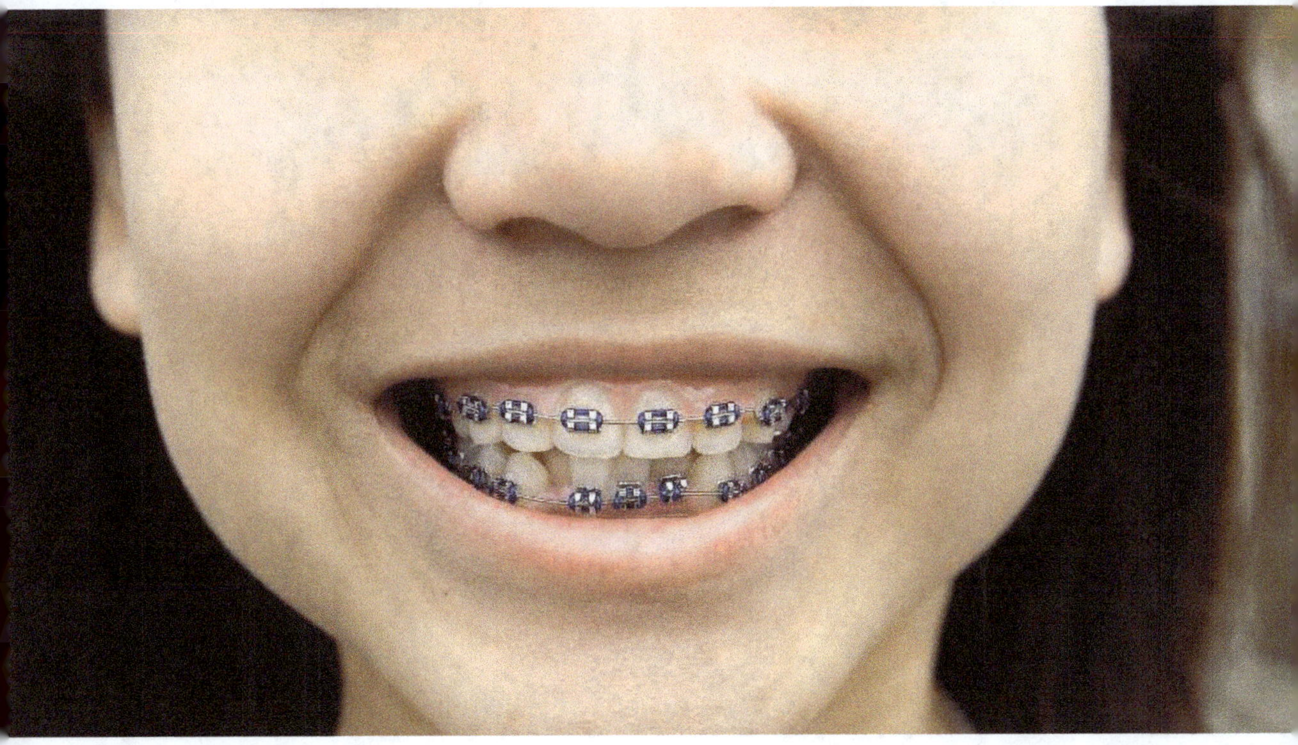

FOOD *for* BRACES

8. Lead by example. Eat your greens and educate the kids about the vitamins and goodness that their body needs while showing them that you are eating yours, let them know healthy food will help them grow smarter, grow stronger and be better at all the things that matter to them.
9. Consider bribery! I paid my son $1 for every brussels sprout he ate one mealtime. He ate ten. He eventually acquired the taste and now as an adult he now eats them happily.

My Philosophy on keeping family harmony at mealtimes

Let them eat what they want! Don't force feed. Dinner time should be about having conversations and enjoying each other's company. Don't turn it into a war zone with penalties and threats of no dessert. That is no fun for anyone. Always keep presenting healthy options. Always keep educating and encouraging. Encouraging is quite different to forcing.

Encouragement could just be 'is today the day you amaze us by eating a green bean?' Believe me, one day you might be surprised!
All the above is a little more complex when kids have braces. They may be more fussy than usual. Their mouth is sore, they are possibly feeling self-conscious, and they are adjusting mentally and physically to a significant change to their body.

Just remember, it is temporary and does not last forever. Be flexible. Be relaxed and supportive. If they only wanted to eat mashed potato. Fine. If they only want ice-cream. Whatever. It is not forever. Ask them what they feel like having, make it for them and make a fuss of them. Everyone loves to be made to feel just a little bit special.

Sample Meal Plan - First Week of Braces

MONDAY	Breakfast	Banana Smoothie
	Lunch	Potato and Leek Soup
	Dinner	Mashed Potatoes and Gravy
	Dessert	Ice cream and jelly
	Snacks	Yoghurt and apple sauce
TUESDAY	Breakfast	Strawberry Smoothie
	Lunch	Potato and Leek Soup (double recipe)
	Dinner	Fish Chowder
	Dessert	Chocolate mousse (store-bought) and jelly
	Snacks	Soft, chopped fruit such as banana, kiwi fruit
WEDNESDAY	Breakfast	Stewed fruit and Yoghurt
	Lunch	Potato and Leek Soup (made yesterday)
	Dinner	Roasted Soft vegies
	Dessert	Ice cream with mashed banana
	Snacks	Vanilla/chocolate cupcake
THURSDAY	Breakfast	Instant Porridge with stewed fruit
	Lunch	Chicken Noodle Soup (double recipe)
	Dinner	Salmon and Pea pasta
	Dessert	Crème caramel (store-bought)
	Snacks	Yoghurt and soft fruit
FRIDAY	Breakfast	Mango Smoothie
	Lunch	Leftover Salmon and pea pasta
	Dinner	Fish Patties and mashed potatoes
	Dessert	Ice cream
	Snacks	Yoghurt and soft fruit
SATURDAY	Breakfast	Banana and cinnamon mash
	Lunch	Chicken Noodle Soup
	Dinner	Savoury Mince and cauliflower cheese
	Dessert	Custard (store-bought) and soft fruit
	Snacks	Yoghurt and apple sauce
SUNDAY	Breakfast	Scrambled eggs
	Lunch	Leftover savoury mince
	Dinner	Sweet Potato, feta, basil pasta salad
	Dessert	Ice cream and soft fruit
	Snacks	Yoghurt and apple sauce

Sample Meal Plan - AFTER First Week of Braces

MONDAY	Breakfast	Pancakes
	Lunch	Leftover Sweet Potato pasta salad
	Dinner	Pulled pork and steamed soft vegetables with butter and pepper
	Dessert	Ice cream
	Snacks	Fruit salad tub (store-bought)
TUESDAY	Breakfast	Smoothie
	Lunch	Ham and cheese Sandwich (cut off crust)
	Dinner	Meatloaf, Mashed Potatoes and Gravy
	Dessert	Ice cream
	Snacks	Muffin
WEDNESDAY	Breakfast	Pikelets with soft fruit
	Lunch	Sandwiches with leftover meatloaf filling
	Dinner	Baked salmon and cauliflower cheese
	Dessert	Chocolate mousse (store-bought) and strawberries
	Snacks	Pikelets
THURSDAY	Breakfast	Mushroom open sandwich
	Lunch	Salmon (leftover) and cheese sandwich
	Dinner	Pan-fried white fish with Potato salad
	Dessert	Apple pudding
	Snacks	Cottage cheese and chopped fruit
FRIDAY	Breakfast	Smoothie of your choice
	Lunch	Potato salad and sliced turkey ribbons
	Dinner	Takeout night! Your choice of a creamy Italian pasta or a tasty Japanese ramen
	Dessert	Apple pudding leftover from last night
	Snacks	Soft pita bread with hummus dip (store-bought)
SATURDAY	Breakfast	Scrambled eggs with salmon
	Lunch	Macaroni cheese
	Dinner	Cottage pie
	Dessert	Apple or Pear crumble
	Snacks	Muffin
SUNDAY	Breakfast	Scrambled eggs
	Lunch	Leftover savoury mince
	Dinner	Sweet Potato, feta, basil pasta salad
	Dessert	Ice cream and soft fruit
	Snacks	Yoghurt and apple sauce

About the Author

Suzanne Burke was born and bred in Perth, Western Australia and has tertiary qualifications in business (information technology) and professional writing. The second half of her career has seen her diversify into roles as a Small Business Manager, Digital Creator, Writer and parent.

Her early career focused within the IT sector with roles as a Computer Programmer, Business Systems Analyst, Technical Writer and Software Tester.

This is the second book for Suzanne. Her first book, **Nail Your Renovation without Getting Screwed**, co-authored with Steve Burke, was published in 2019. This book was the first of its kind in Australia and was a national success story.

The promotional trail for Nail Your Renovation, included being featured on Sunrise TV on Channel 7, The Couch TV, and many radio interviews and podcasts.

Suzanne was also engaged to write a series of feature articles for The West Australian Newspaper, and articles for stacks of magazines including New Idea, Bunnings, Money, Country Style, Your Investment Property, That's Life and Home Design. **FOOD for BRACES** is the second book for Suzanne and fills a void in the market.

Finding information about what to eat and what not to eat when you have braces has until now been information provided by orthodontists. However, this tends to be light on detail and is just a checklist at best. This book provides so much more and ultimately represents the book that Suzanne and her daughter were looking for when Lily's braces journey began.

Getting braces requires adjustments to the way you eat and finding interesting ideas for delicious recipes and knowing what to eat, and what not to eat, is at the heart of this book.

www.ingramcontent.com/pod-product-compliance
Lightning Source LLC
Chambersburg PA
CBHW060533010526
44107CB00059B/2630